AMAZING ANIMALS

Butterflies

Stacy Tornio

muddy boots™

we jump in puddles

Lanham · Boulder · New York · London

Published by Muddy Boots
An Imprint of Globe Pequot
The Rowman & LIttlefield Publishing Group
4501 Forbes Boulevard, Suite 200, Lanham, Maryland 20706
www.rowman.com

Unit A, Whitacre Mews, 26-34 Stannary Street, London, SE11 4AB

Distributed by NATIONAL BOOK NETWORK

Book design by Katie Jennings Design

Photo credits: Variegated fritillary, Bronze copper, Zebra Swallowtail, Cloudless sulphur caterpillar, Smartweed caterpillar, Sulphur male and female, courtesy of Andy Reago & Chrissy McClarren. Gulf Frittillary, Spring Azure, Fiery skipper, Common checkered skipper, Pipevine swallowtail, courtesy of John Flannery. Monarch Egg, Monarch caterpillar, Monarch chrysalis to butterfly, Male monarch, Great spangled fritillary, courtesy of USFWS Midwest. Silver spotted sulphur, Sarah Murray. American copper, Don Henise. Gray Copper, Bob Danely. Eastern Tiger Swallowtail, Chris Sorge. Puddling, Chinmayisk. Puddling, David Hill. Entomologists, USDA. Female monarch, Sid Mosdell.

The National Wildlife Federation & Ranger Rick contributors: Mary Dalheim, John Gallagher, Greg Hudson, Ellen Lambeth, Hannah Schardt, Kathy Kranking, Michele Reyzer, Lori Collins, Cindy Olson, Susan McElhinney, Robyn Gregg, Chris Conway, Deana Duffek, Michael Morris, Kristen Ferriere, David Mizejewski, Maureen Smith.

Thank you for joining the National Wildlife Federation and Muddy Boots in preserving endangered animals and protecting vital wildlife habitats. The National Wildlife Federation is a voice for wildlife protection, dedicated to preserving America's outdoor traditions and inspiring generations of conservationists.

Library of Congress Cataloging-in-Publication Data Available

ISBN 978-1-63076-204-9 (paperback)

ISBN 978-1-63076-205-6 (electronic)

Printed in the United States of America

If you go outside on a bright and sunny day, there's a good chance you're going to see some butterflies. They love hanging out in the sun!

Now, when you think of a butterfly, you probably imagine a beautiful swallowtail or a popular monarch. Both of these are common butterflies that you can see in your backyard and neighborhood, but there are many other types (called *species*) that you can also see. In fact, more than seven hundred different types of butterflies are found in North America alone. Let's start learning about these beautiful creatures of the insect family!

Baltimore checkerspot

CATERPILLARS

BUTTERFLIES TEND TO GET ALL THE ATTENTION because they are bigger and often more colorful, but don't overlook caterpillars. They're cool, too! Think of caterpillars as the baby form of butterflies and moths. They are actually called *larvae* (lahr-vuh). It might be tempting to call them worms, but they're not. Although they may look a little worm-like, take a closer look and you'll see that they have a segmented body, and underneath, little legs.

Caterpillars are often hard to see because they can be very, very tiny. This is because they hatch from a butterfly egg, which can be smaller than the head of a pin. So they start off really little, but then they eat lots of plant material, making them grow bigger very quickly. As the caterpillar gets larger, it will shed its skin several times. Once it reaches full size, it will stop eating and make a new home for itself out of hardened protein, called *exoskeleton*. This new home is a *chrysalis* (kris-uh-lis), which the caterpillar usually attaches to the underside of the leaf where it was eating. Now its job is done!

Black swallowtail caterpillar

Spicebush swallowtail caterpillar

BUTTERFLIES

MANY TIMES PEOPLE FORGET THAT BUTTERFLIES ARE PART OF THE INSECT FAMILY, but they have a head, thorax, and abdomen just like other insects.

Think about the colors on a butterfly for a second. Believe it or not, these colorful patterns are actually like tiny little scales—a lot like the scales on a fish—except they are soft and feathery. In fact, the official name scientists use to classify butterflies and moths is *Lepidoptera* (lep-i-dop-ter-uh), which means "scaly wings" in Latin. This makes them pretty special, because they are the only insects that have scales on their bodies!

Butterflies can vary a great deal in size. They might be less than an inch, or several inches wide—even more if their wings are spread out. Don't be overwhelmed by all the different types of butterflies out there. It's fun to learn about them because then you can look for different species when you're out and about, exploring the outdoors.

Viceroy

Western swallowtail

Common sulphur

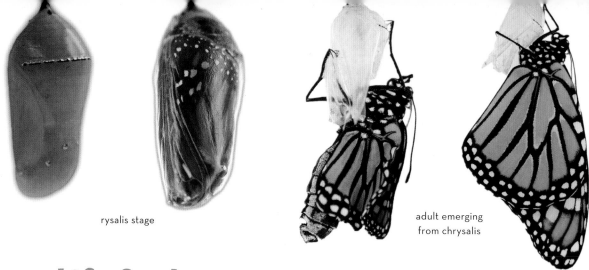

rysalis stage

adult emerging
from chrysalis

Life Cycle

The life cycle of a butterfly is truly one of the most amazing things in nature. It's amazing to think about a teeny, tiny egg transforming into a butterfly in just a few short weeks! To understand how it happens, it's important to look at each of the four stages of the life cycle:

- **Egg:** Female butterflies usually lay their eggs on plant leaves. They can lay one hundred eggs or more. Inside each egg is a tiny little caterpillar that will hatch in about three to five days.

- **Caterpillar:** Once the caterpillar hatches (this is also called the *larva stage*), the little caterpillar starts eating so it can grow and keep shedding its skin. This goes on for a week or two. Then when the caterpillar is done growing, it finds a good place to rest.

- **Chrysalis:** Also called the *pupa* (pyoo-puh), the chrysalis has an important job. Sure, it just sits there, but this is where the astonishing transformation starts to happen. The caterpillar is turning into a butterfly! This stage takes another week or two.

- **Butterfly:** Once the chrysalis cracks open, the butterfly starts to emerge. It might take only a few minutes for this to happen. Then the butterfly waits while its wings dry. A few hours later, the butterfly takes off, ready to find food from flowers. In a couple of weeks, it'll start looking for a place to lay its eggs, and the entire cycle starts all over again.

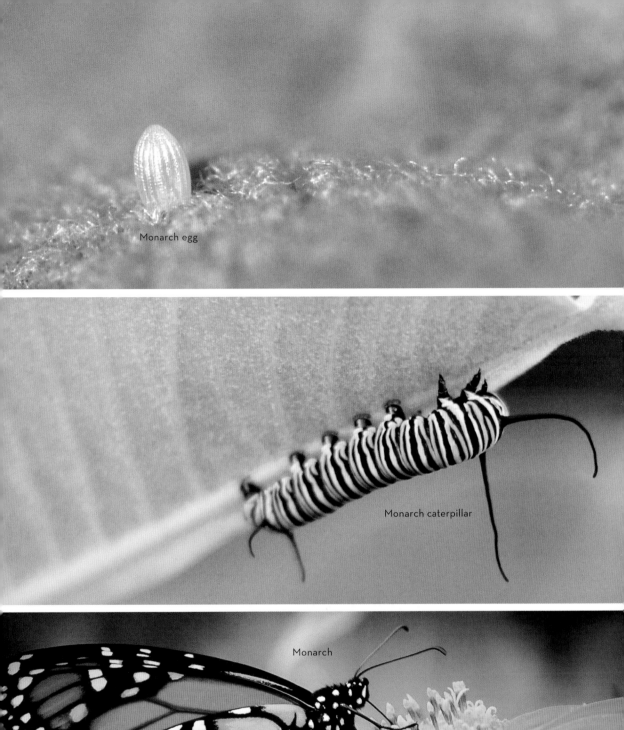

Monarch egg

Monarch caterpillar

Monarch

Butterfly proboscis

Eating Habits

To understand this insect's eating habits, you have to break it down into the caterpillar stage and the butterfly stage. First, caterpillars eat lots and lots of plant leaves. If you've ever seen a leaf after a caterpillar has been at it, you'll notice that there are lots of holes. This is because they are constantly eating!

Once the butterfly hatches, it's off to look for food from flowers. It needs this food in liquid form. In order to get it, the butterfly uses its interesting tongue, called a *proboscis*. It's a lot like a straw, and the butterfly sucks up nectar with it. Sometimes they'll even stop and sip on some juices from fruits. Have you ever seen a butterfly feeder? You can make your own with a mixture of sugar and water (there are good instructions online for making one). As the butterfly goes from flower to flower, it's also doing a very important job: helping to pollinate flowers, just like bees do.

American lady

Cloudless sulphur caterpillar

Defenses

Think about caterpillars and butterflies for a minute. They're pretty small, right? Plus, they're quite fragile. Even those little, bitty eggs—how do they survive?

It's easy to think that caterpillars and butterflies don't have many defenses, but they do have a few tricks. Here are four main ways they defend themselves:

Smart weed caterpillar

1. Poison. Caterpillars and butter-flies don't produce their own poison, but some of the plants they eat contain poison. While the insects are unaffected by the poison, they become poisonous to the bigger animals that want to eat them.

2. Camouflage. Butterflies and caterpillars often have colors or patterns that help them blend in with their surroundings. This means that predators like birds, frogs, and other small animals don't eat them, because they can't really see them!

3. Eyespots. Both caterpillars and butterflies can have *eyespots*. These are just markings on the bodies or wings that look like two eyes—a trick to make them look like a larger animal.

4. Spines and smells. Some cater-pillars have stinging spines that they use to discourage predators from trying to eat them. Others have glands that let off a strong odor to keep predators and parasites away!

Monarch

Threats and Conservation

Did you know that the monarch butterfly population is actually in decline? It's true. There just aren't as many monarchs around as there used to be, due to things like loss of habitat and more people using pesticides. (Pesticides that are made to kill weeds also destroy the milkweed plants where the monarchs lay their eggs; this, in turn, harms the butterflies.) It's not just monarchs, either. Many other butterfly species are also seeing a decline.

So what's the answer? How can you help? First of all, you can talk about the dangers of pesticides, urging those around you to cut back, or not to use them at all. They are harmful to butterflies, birds, and other animals. In addition, you can provide special gardens for butterflies (more on that in the next section). And finally, you can help spread the word. A big part of conservation is just sharing what you know with others. Tell your family and friends that the monarch population is actually in trouble; most people don't even realize this. Education is definitely needed, and this is something you can help with at any time.

Learn more about how you can help at: RangerRick.com and search Butterfly.

GARDENING for Butterflies

When it comes to gardening for butterflies, there are two main kinds of plants you want to be aware of. The first is host plants, and the second is nectar plants.

Host Plants

Many caterpillars can only eat a few types of plants. In the case of the monarch, they only eat milkweed plants. These are called *host plants*, and it's very important that they are available. If a butterfly can't find a specific host plant on which to lay her eggs, then those little caterpillars aren't going to survive because they will not have the food they need to eat. You can do your part by learning about different host plants, especially for the common butterflies in your area. Everyone should plant milkweed, though. If more people did this, it would help the monarch population overall.

Nectar Plants

Most butterflies need *nectar plants*—plants that create a sweet sugary liquid that butterflies and other animals drink. You can try zinnias from seed, or for perennials (which means they'll come back every year), try bee balm. It's a great nectar plant! These are just the beginning. Ask your local nursery or gardening friend about some other good choices for butterfly plants in your area.

Monarch feeding on milkweed

Fritillary

Bring on the BUTTERFLIES

When flowers bloom, butterflies won't be far behind. Try these ideas for a summer of butterfly fun!

Welcome Garden

A butterfly garden is a place butterflies love to flutter to. It takes just a few things to make one in your yard. (No yard? How about a balcony, a window box, or your school grounds?)

Here's what you'll need

- **Nectar flowers.** Plant colorful, sweet-smelling flowers with flat tops. Butterflies will come flocking to sip nectar.

- **Host plants for caterpillars.** Caterpillars grow up to be butterflies (or moths) so include some plants that caterpillars eat.

- **Puddling areas.** Fill a shallow pan with wet sand or mud. Butterflies may land here to collect minerals as they sip.

- **Basking rocks.** Add a few rocks to give butterflies a place to rest and warm up in the sun.

Tiger swallowtail

Tiger swallowtail

Fritillary

Red admirals

Tips for Butterfly Success

- Plant your garden in a sunny spot that's also sheltered from the wind.

- Group plants so that lots of flowers grow close together.

- Choose a variety of plants that bloom at different times. That will keep your butterfly café open through spring, summer, and early fall.

- Don't use pesticides. They're bad for butterflies—and for people and pets, too!

BUTTERFLY STUDIES

Once butterflies have arrived, sit back and enjoy the show! If your winged visitors are willing, you might also want to investigate some of these questions:

- **Make a Menu.** Which flowers are most popular? Check out whether certain kinds of butterflies seem to prefer visiting certain flowers.

- **Look Hard.** Do the butterflies' colors blend in or stand out? Are they more camouflaged with their wings open or closed?

- **Take Roll.** Can you identify the butterflies you spot? Note their size and shape, the colors and patterns on their wings, and how they fly. Then use a field guide to search for their names. You could also go online to **butterfliesandmoths.org** for lots of helpful information.

- **Zoom In.** Can you get close enough to watch a butterfly's long tongue unroll? Can you use a magnifying glass to see the tiny scales that cover its wings?

- **Get the Shot.** Will your favorite butterflies pose for a photo? Snap some pictures and frame the best ones or make a book to show them off.

Pansy

Queen Anne's lace

Red clover

Parsley

Sage

Yarrow

Aster

Bee balm

Black-eyed Susan

Butterfly weed

Dill

Hyssop

Lupine

Marigold

Milkweed

Mint

Best plants for NECTARS

Cosmos

Aster

Zinnia

Bee balm

Marigold

Butterfly weed

Red clover

Sage

Mint

Black-eyed Susan

Purple coneflower

Best plants for CATERPILLARS

Milkweed

Dill

Parsley

Yarrow

Lupine

Queen Anne's lace

Pansy

Hyssop

Thyme

MOTHS

At first glance, a moth can look like a butterfly and a butterfly can look like a moth. They are in the same main scientific order, *Lepidoptera*, but there are several differences.

First, most moths are *nocturnal*, which means they fly at night, while most butterflies are active during the day. (This isn't always true, however; a few moths are active during the day, too.)

Second, moths have feathery antennas, while butterflies have tiny little "clubs" at the end of theirs.

Third, butterflies and moths position their wings differently when they are resting. Here's a quick tip that can help you identify which is which, from a distance: Butterflies often fold their wings up vertically when they're at rest, while moths will spread theirs out.

Fourth, and last, moths come from cocoons, a covering made from silk threads. Moth caterpillars weave the cocoon when they enter the pupa phase. A lot of people say butterflies come from cocoons, but as you learned earlier, they *pupate* in a chrysalis. Many people don't know this; test it out on your friends!

Overall, moths are really fascinating. In fact, a hobby called "mothing" is really becoming popular. People put out a black light (bright white lights will work, too) in front of a white sheet with some liquid bait or food on it. They do this at night during the summer and then wait. Once the moths come up to the light and land on the sheet, you can get a nice, close-up look. Then all you need is a good moth book, and you can start to identify them!

Cecropia moths

Luna moth

AMAZING FACTS

Increase your caterpillar and butterfly knowledge with these fifteen amazing facts. They're perfect for testing out on your friends.

1. Butterflies use their feet to taste with.

2. They will sometimes gather at mud puddles and sip nutrients from the soil. This is called *puddling*.

3. When butterflies overwinter, they usually do it in the chrysalis stage. They'll stay there until spring.

4. Monarchs are unique when it comes to how they spend their winters, as they are one of the only butterflies that migrate. Most of them go down to Mexico.

5. A butterfly needs to be warm. In fact, its body temperature needs to be 86 degrees Fahrenheit in order to fly.

6. Want to tell the difference between a male and a female monarch? Males have a little dot along the lower part of their wings; you can see this on both sides. Females lack this spot.

7. Most butterflies live only two to four weeks total.

8. The top speed for most butterflies is about 12 miles per hour.

9. Someone who studies insects, including butterflies, is called an *entomologist*.

10. Butterflies (and all insects) have their skeleton on the outside of their bodies instead of the inside. This is called an *exoskeleton*.

Swallowtails puddling.

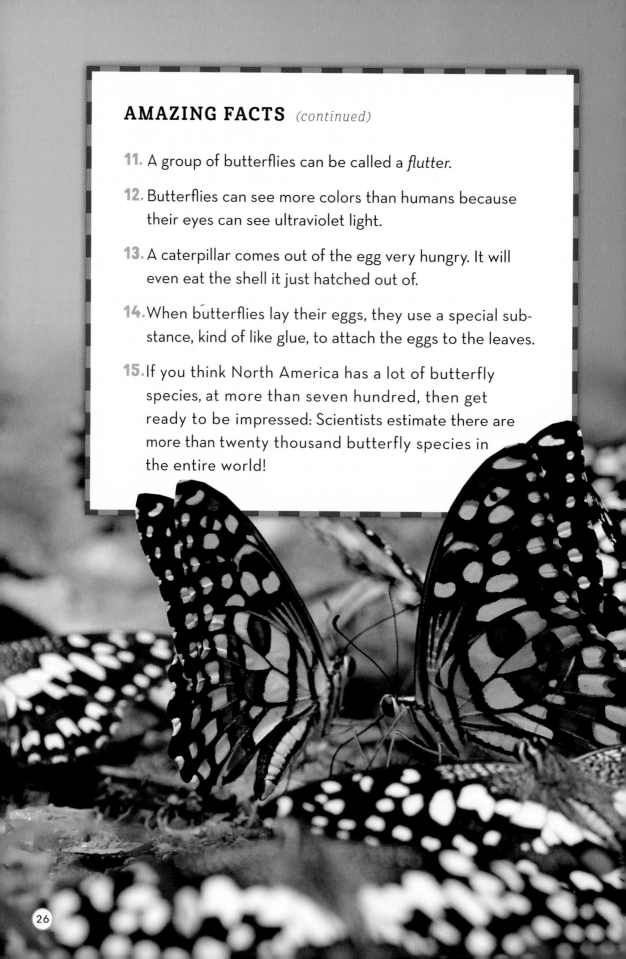

AMAZING FACTS *(continued)*

11. A group of butterflies can be called a *flutter*.

12. Butterflies can see more colors than humans because their eyes can see ultraviolet light.

13. A caterpillar comes out of the egg very hungry. It will even eat the shell it just hatched out of.

14. When butterflies lay their eggs, they use a special substance, kind of like glue, to attach the eggs to the leaves.

15. If you think North America has a lot of butterfly species, at more than seven hundred, then get ready to be impressed: Scientists estimate there are more than twenty thousand butterfly species in the entire world!

FIELD GUIDE

With so many different types of butterflies in North America, it's important to know what to look for when you're outside. This way you can start telling the difference between species. Here are a few butterfly groups to keep an eye out for when you're outside on a sunny day.

SWALLOWTAILS

They are some of the largest butterflies in North America, ranging from two to five inches. Most have a yellow-and-black pattern, but some species are mostly black all over. Look for:

- **Eastern tiger swallowtail**
- **Western tiger swallowtail**
- **Zebra swallowtail**
- **Giant swallowtail**
- **Pipevine swallowtail**

Western tiger swallowtail

Eastern tiger swallowtail

Zebra swallowtail

Giant swallowtail

Pipevine swallowtail

Monarch

MONARCHS AND MIMICS

The monarch is one of the most recognized butterflies in the world, with its orange-and-black pattern. Two other species that look like the monarch (called *mimics*) are the queen and the viceroy. All are about three to four inches in size. Since the queen and the viceroy look like monarchs—poisonous to predators because they eat milkweed—predators think they are also poisonous, and avoid them. Look for:

- **Monarch**
- **Viceroy**
- **Queen**

Viceroy

Queen

BLUES AND COPPERS

While these are some of the smallest butterflies in North America, they are so much fun! Some of them can be smaller than an inch, but don't overlook them! Once you take a closer look, you'll see just how beautiful they are, and how intriguing their patterns can be. Look for:

- **Eastern tailed-blue**
- **American copper**
- **Spring azure**
- **Gray copper**
- **Bronze copper**

Eastern tailed-blue

Spring azure

Bronze copper

Gray copper

American copper

Small copper

FRITILLARIES

Once you learn to recognize one fritillary, you can learn them all. Like other butterfly groups, they have similar patterns and shapes when they are perched at a flower. They aren't as big as swallowtails, but the larger ones can have a wing span of 4 inches. It won't be long before you can easily pick them out when they're flying. Look for:

- **Great spangled fritillary**
- **Variegated fritillary**
- **Gulf fritillary**

Gulf fritillary

Great spangled fritillary

Variegated fritillary

Least skipper

SKIPPERS

Also on the small side, these butterflies range in size from just a half-inch to an inch and a half. They get their name because they tend to "skip" around from one flower to the next. They are always on the move, going really fast. This means you'll have to be quick if you want to see one. Sometimes skippers have plain, darker colors, but don't think they're boring. With more than two hundred different species in North America, they are easy to find and really fun to watch. Look for:

- **Silver-spotted skipper**
- **Least skipper**
- **Common checkered-skipper**
- **Fiery skipper**

Silver-spotted skipper

Common checkered-skipper

Fiery skipper

Clouded sulphur

WHITES AND SULPHURS

Both of these are in the same family of
butterflies. They are small fliers that
really like open fields. They aren't very
big—only about one to two inches.
Since they usually keep their wings
folded up when they're perched,
wait for them to take off. When
they're flying, you can see their
colorful undersides. Look for:

· **Cabbage white**

· **Checkered white**

· **Clouded sulphur**

· **Orange sulphur**

· **Southern dogface**

Cabbage white

Common sulphur

Southern dogface

Checkered white

Orange sulphur

Author: STACY TORNIO

Question: Do you see a lot of butterflies where you live? What kind?

Answer: I love looking for butterflies in my backyard and at local parks. My favorite butterfly is the Mourning cloak. This is one of the first ones to come out in spring, and it always makes me happy when I see one. Then I know that warmer days are ahead!

National Wildlife Federation Naturalist: DAVID MIZEJEWSKI

Question: Do you see a lot of butterflies where you live? What kind?

Answer: I have lots of butterflies in my yard including Swallowtails, Sulphers, Admirals, Monarchs, and Skippers. I've planted lots of flowering plants to provide nectar and host plants for caterpillars to eat.

Illustrator (Ranger Rick & Scarlett Fox characters): PARKER JACOBS

Question: What butterfly color or pattern is your favorite?

Answer: Although the monarch butterfly is the most popular wing pattern, I love the pleated pattern and shape of a Mormon butterfly.